PECULIAR PETS

Poetic Verse

Edited By Sarah Waterhouse

First published in Great Britain in 2021 by:

Young Writers
Remus House
Coltsfoot Drive
Peterborough
PE2 9BF
Telephone: 01733 890066
Website: www.youngwriters.co.uk

Book Design by Ashley Janson

Softback ISBN 978-1-80015-160-4

Printed and bound in the UK by BookPrintingUK
Website: www.bookprintinguk.com
YB0455D

FOREWORD

Welcome Reader!

Are you ready to discover weird and wonderful creatures that you'd never even dreamed of?

For Young Writers' latest competition we asked primary school pupils to create a Peculiar Pet of their own invention, and then write a poem about it! They rose to the challenge magnificently and the result is this fantastic collection full of creepy critters and amazing animals!

Here at Young Writers our aim is to encourage creativity in children and to inspire a love of the written word, so it's great to get such an amazing response, with some absolutely fantastic poems. Not only have these young authors created imaginative and inventive animals, they've also crafted wonderful poems to showcase their creations and their writing ability. These poems are brimming with inspiration. The slimiest slitherers, the creepiest crawlers and furriest friends are all brought to life in these pages – you can decide for yourself which ones you'd like as a pet!

I'd like to congratulate all the young authors in this anthology, I hope this inspires them to continue with their creative writing.

★ CONTENTS ★

Rawcliffe Primary School, Rawcliffe

Sebert Wood Community Primary School, Bury St Edmunds

St Bernadette's Catholic Primary School, Birmingham

Daisy Tilley (8)	156
Joyce Biniam (8)	157
Abigail Bovas (9)	158
Zunariah (8)	159
Lexie Walsh (8)	160
Alfie Russell (9)	161
Kelvin Mutebi Wamala (8)	162
Harrison Plant (9)	163
Cassie-Jo Smith-Silver (8)	164
Greta Raubiska (8)	165
Sophie Bromage (8)	166
Connor Watkins (8)	167
Adeena Anjum (8)	168
Isam Malik (8)	169
Jersey Kinnelly (8)	170

Swaffham Bulbeck CE Primary School, Swaffham Bulbeck

Jayden Wong (8)	171
Tanaka Mafuva (7)	172
Sophie Blundell (8)	173
K Stanyer (8)	174
Joshua Parker (8)	176
Avah Bailey (7)	177
Oliver Arksey (8)	178
Joshua Hedges (7)	179
Jess Barber (7)	180
Xavier Kirkby (8)	181
Melody Speed (7)	182
Amber Smith (8)	183
Oscar Deistler (7)	184
Hazel Weaver (9)	185
Molly Sutherland (8)	186
Sophie Fenton (7)	187
Sidney Riethoff (8)	188
Flossie (7)	189
Fred Fernandez (8)	190
Noah Poujardieu (7)	191
Hester Rudkin (8)	192
Sophie Grant Berry (8)	193

William MacGregor Primary School, Tamworth

Makenzie Hope (9)	194
Amelia Watson (7)	195
Lydia Dennis (9)	196
Alfie Allen (7)	197

THE POEMS

Owler (Owl And Deer)

He stumbles when he walks
And he toots when he talks.

He whirls and turns around
Making a hooting sound.

He likes to fly and sit on branches
But because of his antlers he is too heavy.

His legs he misses for escaping
But owl legs are fun for perching.

An Owler has two wings, nice.
I wonder if he can still hunt mice?

Tikshna Mewada (8)
Balgreen Primary School, Edinburgh

Owly (Owl And Butterfly)

He flutters when he walks
And he hoots when he talks
He flies and flaps around
Making a tooting sound.
He likes to stay awake at night
But he's scared of the dark
His feathers he misses for sweeping the sky
But patterns are fun for decorating wings
An Owly has two hairy legs
I wonder if it could still eat meat?

Mahera Kashif (8)
Balgreen Primary School, Edinburgh

Zebfish (Zebra And Fish)

He swims when he walks
And he bubbles when he talks
He flaps and jumps around
Making a splashing sound
He likes to run but he has no legs
Stripes are good for looking nice
His tail he misses for swishing off flies
But fins are fun for water, not skies
A Zebfish has no grinding teeth
I wonder if he can move on land.

Oushneek Dey (7)

Balgreen Primary School, Edinburgh

Birsnail (Bird And Snail)

He flies around when he walks
And he chirps when he talks
He flaps his wings and slimes around
Making a cheeping sound
He likes to hide in his shell
As he can't walk very well
His feathers he misses for keeping him warm
But long eyes are fun for seeing things
A Birsnail has a beak
I wonder if it can still lay eggs?

Ruby Law (8)
Balgreen Primary School, Edinburgh

Beetsnail (Beetle And Snail)

He slides when he walks
And he scratches when he talks.
He rolls and feels around
Making a slurping sound.
He cannot glide but he likes to hide
It is fun to crawl and slide.
His legs he misses for running away
But a foot is fun for wiggling.
A Beetsnail has a shell and slime
I wonder if it can still fly high.

Beth Stuart (8)

Balgreen Primary School, Edinburgh

The Woodat (Woodlouse And Cat)

It limps when it walks
And it meows when it talks.
It leaps and climbs around
Making a purring sound.
It likes to hide but whenever it tries
It can't dig holes nearby.
Its antennae it misses for sensing things.
But designs are fun for bling!
A Woodat has a long tail.
I wonder if it is as slow as a snail!

Siya Patil (8)
Balgreen Primary School, Edinburgh

Zebee (Bee And Zebra)

He tries to fly when he walks
And goes buzzy when he talks.
He hovers and stumbles around
Making a bumbling sound.
He likes long grass for grazing
But to make honey is amazing.
His wings he misses for gliding
But legs are fun for striding.
A Zebee has stripes, not wings.
I wonder if he still stings?

Iona Day (8)
Balgreen Primary School, Edinburgh

The Dogbir (Dog And Bird)

He flies when he walks
And he woofs when he talks.
He flaps and glides around
Making a pecking sound.
He likes to eat a lot
But sometimes he gets a tummy ache.
His beak he misses for getting worms
But tongues are fun for licking.
A Dogbir has four furry legs
I wonder if it can still dig up bones?

Eva Lizdenyte (8)
Balgreen Primary School, Edinburgh

A Cadot (Cat And Dog)

He sneaks when he walks
And he wags his tongue when he talks
He scratches and miaows around
Making a barking sound
He likes to play in snow
But he can't climb trees
His eyes he misses for night vision
But his legs are fun for running
A Cadot has a long tail
I wonder if he can still pounce?

Madaa Alm Alsalem (8)
Balgreen Primary School, Edinburgh

The Cabird (Cat And Bird)

He pounces when he walks
And he miaows when he talks.
He glides and leaps around
Making a squawking sound.
He likes to fly
But for cats it's too high.
His four feet he misses for running fast
But his wings are fun for flying past.
A Cabird has no tail of fur
I wonder if it can still purr?

Kya Robertson-Calder (8)
Balgreen Primary School, Edinburgh

Douse (Dog Mouse)

He sprints when he walks
And he squeaks when he talks
He lurks and runs around
Making a barking sound
He likes to climb
But whenever he tries, he fails
His nose he misses for sniffing for food
But long legs are fun for running fast
A Douse has a pink nose
I wonder if it can still jump high.

Clara Milano (8)
Balgreen Primary School, Edinburgh

The Dosh (Dog And Fish)

He wiggles when he walks
And he barks when he talks
He paddles and swims around
Making a splashing sound
He likes to run and jump
But when he tries, he falls over
His back legs he misses for playing catch
But flippers are fun for flapping
A Dosh has an orange fin
I wonder if it can swim.

Laila Ferguson (8)
Balgreen Primary School, Edinburgh

Best Friend's Tale

Quietly scuttling in their cage,
Willow and Phoebe are in a rage
Desperately trying to get out of the shop
And disappear through the rooftop,
Whiskers twitching, paws clawing,
The two little friends find it boring
To stay and be laughed at all day long,
With big round eyes and a smelly pong,
Their smooth long tails attract a crowd,
Now they will do something that's not allowed
And sneak out into the dead of night,
While everyone's snuggled up tight.
What a special night it turned out to be,
A white-gloved hand came and set them free,
A big jolly fellow led them onto a sleigh...
And the majestic antlered beasts took them up, up and away,
Through the starry night they soared,
Until they stopped at a white front door,
Finally placed into their new nest,
To hear in the morning, "They are the best!"

Kieran Holmes (10)

Christ The King Catholic Primary School, Bromborough

Peculiar Pet

I'd like to tell you a tale of my particularly peculiar pet,
It's not the type of pet that you would take to the vet,
It all started on a blustery bleak beach,
When I stumbled across a strange speckled rock that was just out of my reach,
I looked around
Until I found
An old fishing net
That I stretched and stretched until I was covered in sweat,
I finally got the strange speckled rock
And dried it off with my smelly old sock.

I headed home with my find under my coat,
I put it in the bath where it began to float,
I washed it off only to discover
I'd taken an egg away from its mother!
I wrapped it in a warm blanket to keep it safe and sound,
Then it grew and grew until it weighed over fifty pounds.

Some cracks appeared in the old speckled shell
And it began to give off an unusual smell,
Then the old speckled egg finally hatched,
Out came a dragon, it leaned over and snatched
The food off my plate, it all disappeared,
It was worse than I thought, even worse than I feared.

I mean a *dragon*,
A red fire-breathing dragon!
I panicked like crazy for I was shocked and surprised,
Then it turned around and looked me straight in the eyes...

I looked through the history books but there was no dragon in sight,
So I went on the computer and searched for dragons, in fright,
There were only tales in fairy books and myths from lands far away,

But one book was quite helpful, on the ancient pages it did say
The secret to raising a dragon is love and desire,
Most importantly of all, to stay away from the fire!

Charlie Lewis (10)
Christ The King Catholic Primary School, Bromborough

Bella The Bunny

B eyond beautiful bunny,
E legant, fluffy bunny and never gets hurt,
L ate sometimes but is very silly,
L azy but still cuddly,
A ddicted to noodles called 'Mr Noodles',

T eo comes and Bella only eats peas for tea,
H er mum always comes and tucks her in for bed,
E very day she gets up at 11am and hops downstairs for breakfast,

B ella goes out on a Friday to watch her cousin play football,
"U ndo your shoes," says Mum after Bella's walk,
"N o!" shouts Mum when Bella's big brother asks for food before breakfast,
"N ot today," says Bella's mum when Bella asks to go on a walk,
"Y ou are the best bunny," Bella's mum says every day, every hour.

Bella Hall (9)
Christ The King Catholic Primary School, Bromborough

My Amazing Pugicorn

Yesterday, I adopted an amazing pet called a Pugicorn
When I got home, I began wondering
What does my pet like?
I fed my pet, lots of things were in sight
I wanted to know, was my pet nice?

When I stroked my pet, wings sprang out
So I went outside and hopped on my awesome pet
Quickly, we flew up
I was amazed but also really frightened

Suddenly, we began to go down
We crashed down on the ground
I hurt myself and was so surprised to feel pain
She started to run as fast as a cheetah
With me on her back.

I thought I should go for a walk
So I left my pet behind
When I came back from a great walk
My mischievous pet had thrown a party!

I began to get everyone out
Once everyone was out
I wanted to teach my pet tricks
So I found my great pet and went outside
I wondered what tricks it already knew

When we were at the park
My cute flying pet jumped with excitement
She swung on the long swings
She went down the slide
I was glad I had a
Great, naughty pet.

Tara Madden (8)
Christ The King Catholic Primary School, Bromborough

Bob The Crocodile

P lunging into the water, ready to slaughter some fish, was Bob the crocodile.
E ating fish ravenously, wishing gloomily that his friends would come back.
C rying, he said, "I wish they would come back." They left him because he's not on the same track.
U nderneath the water he dived, he was quite unlike the others, he had special powers.
L iving alone was hard, his special power was that he could fly far.
I ndeed he could fly, but his friends had gone far away.
A distance unreachable they went, hunters were around to murder...
R ound the bushes, rustling was heard, Bob knew there was a hunter...

P laced in the bushes was a sniper zooming in on
Bob the crocodile...
E ventually, the rustling stopped and a scream
was heard from the bush.
T hen out came his friends, they weren't mean,
they were just hiding from hunters!
S topping what he was doing, he smiled, he was
back living with his kind, caring friends that
stayed with him all along...

Alex Crosby (10)
Christ The King Catholic Primary School, Bromborough

The D Wolf

My pet is no ordinary pet
That you'd take to the vet.
My pet is a very strange pet
That that you wouldn't ever take to the vet!
It all started out when I was in the forest,
When I saw a strange rock
Bobbing by the crystal-blue river.
Clutching my bag,
I came closer until I reached the rock,
I held out my hand and picked it up,
The car was parked nearby
I put the rock at the back
I thought it was a seed at the back.
I was soon home
But little did I know
It was an egg.
A few hours passed
The weird seed started moving and a piece fell off!
A tail came out,
Soon wings and the body.

A D Wolf,
It couldn't be,
I had something.
I went to the books to find facts
But they were only in fiction books and fairy tales,
They are magical creatures
As fast as a cheetah with wings,
What to do?

Olivia Trinidad (8)
Christ The King Catholic Primary School, Bromborough

What Is The Most Peculiar Pet?

There are many peculiar pets
Like the Spaghetia Spaniel who has no fur
But has a Spaghetia coat
And if you dare
Beware
He does not tend to share his fur
Not many are as strange as the stretchy sausage dog
This fantastic creature can stretch to be
The length of five football pitches.
However, neither of them are as bizarre
As the giant buffalo bulldog
Who can eat two tonnes of food in a day
And weigh
A shocking two kilograms after it's had its meal!
This, however, is the most fantastic, extraordinary creature of all
But sadly it went extinct back in 1575
It was called the dragonfly
I know what you're thinking

They're alive now and they're not that strange
But this species could breathe fire
And set itself on fire
But it was scared of pigs
Shockingly, they ate wombats.

Riley Mohammed (10)
Christ The King Catholic Primary School, Bromborough

Fifi The Talented Sausage Fox

Fifi the cheeky,
Fifi the posh,
You'll know when you're with her
Because she is a tap-dancing sausage fox.
If you are wondering what she's doing
Then don't bother,
She is totally amazing
But can fight like a sister and a brother.

Fifi is as furry as a polar bear,
She is very unique and that is rare.
When she eats food,
She always needs a napkin
Even if it's doughnuts with jam in.
Fifi never makes a mistake
Especially when she is cutting a yummy cake.
At parties, she is as sassy as a little girl.
She dances around and does a huge twirl.

Sometimes, other dogs call Fifi mean
But I would prefer to call her the queen.
When she is tired, she goes to bed
Then she wakes up and has a sore head.
Suddenly, she gets in a mood
And then starts eating all of the food!

Tasmin Greve (8)
Christ The King Catholic Primary School, Bromborough

A True Story

There was a dog called Dipper,
She'd never nip ya.
She's a Jack Russel that is energectic,
Her personality is magnetic.
She's very loud
And very proud.
Cuddle her, snuggle her, it never gets old
Do it as much as you want as it's starting to get cold.
She's a playful little pup, she never gets tired.
She loves a good stroke
But not from any old bloke,
She hates a soak
Especially if there's a smell of smoke.
We would never swap her
As we chose to adopt her.
Her name is Dipper
She always pinches Mum's slippers.
She's my cute little buddy
That hates getting muddy.

She's kind and sweet,
The kinda dog you'd love to meet!
She's my best snuggle buddy
She has a great big heart,
But never stand behind her as she might...

Elizabeth Wilson (11)

Christ The King Catholic Primary School, Bromborough

There's A Snoofer In My House!

There's a Snoofer in my house,
It's louder than a mouse,
I saw it bounce around my room
And heard its loud roar boom.

It flaps its purple wings
And knocks Mum's shiny rings,
Mum likes its green high heels,
But it slips in orange peels!

I tell it to find its own way,
But it comes back to my room straight away,
Sometimes I think it looks funny,
It really doesn't look like a bunny.

It has red spots on its wings
Which knock Mum's rings
And enormous feet
Which dance to the beat.

Then one night we had a movie night
With popcorn and before I took a bite,
I sat with the Snoofer that was in my house,
That now was as quiet as a mouse.

So actually,
I like a Snoofer being in my house after all!

Noah Howard (10)

Christ The King Catholic Primary School, Bromborough

Bob My Marvellous, Extraordinary Goldfish

Bob, my marvellous, extraordinary goldfish, plays in goal
You will find him practising in his bowl!

When the ball comes in, he dives for the save
I think he's incredibly brave.

Most goalkeepers have hands and feet
But even with his flippers he's hard to beat.

He can whack the ball hard but it still travels slow
The water tank stops it from its speedy flow.

He wears a flat cap like my friend Yashin
He has his own crazy fashion!
I think he looks smashin'.

The crowd goes wild as he parries it away
The corals in his tank start to sway.

He gets his oxygen through his gills
And uses his skills to pay the bills.

At the end of the day, it's just me and him
We chill out together as he polishes his fin.

Michael Phelan (10)

Christ The King Catholic Primary School, Bromborough

The Yoghurt Dog

Where does your favourite snack come from?
A cupboard or a shelf,
The fridge or a pack?
My favourite snack comes from the fridge...

In the fridge
There lives a yoghurt dog
That really avoids jumping off the ridge,
Because down below is a hard bog.

There is another pet that lives in the house, that is really fat,
It's the old and lazy house cat.
He would really like to eat the dog,
Just like he did to the baby frog, wait...
That cat really is a meanie!

The yoghurt dog really wants to play for Liverpool FC,
Although he thinks he would be sold for free.
The yoghurt dog is really small,
When he plays netball, he always stalls.

But I think it's time to say goodbye,
So that I can feed the lazy cat some meaty pie.

Liam Carter (10)

Christ The King Catholic Primary School, Bromborough

Georgia The Unigiraffe

Georgia has a glowing glam dress.
She has swimming shoes as shiny as the sun.
Posing for pics, by the time it is done
She will shout, "I've had such fun!"

Georgia's horns can grant magical wishes
But be aware, she does not like washing dishes.
If she can't have her way, she will throw a fit.

Georgia likes to play in the sandpit
She slays then runs away
And she only works in the day.

She rides in a limo
"Off to bingo," she tells her driver
"Drop me off and I'll go,"
But he says, "No!"

Her house is as big as President Trump's
Don't get in a fight
Or she might bite

She can sprint as fast as a cheetah
But sometimes is as slow as a snail.

Zoe Evans (9)
Christ The King Catholic Primary School, Bromborough

The Rainbow Flamingo

T he flamingo is snoring while the sun is rising.
H ow long will it take to wake up?
E arly in the morning she is finally awake, to play along all day

R unning or waddling
A mazing, she is red, orange, yellow, green, blue, purple, like a rainbow
I n the morning, she is going for a swim
N o, there is a shark!
B ut she is okay.
O n Tuesday, she's going to the city
W alking through the city

F lamingo trying to find a friend
L ucky me!
A s bossy as a parent but as kind as a friend
M essy is her room
I ncredible find
N o, don't go
G oing to my room now
O n Wednesday I will see you again, bye for now.

Sophie Mcknight (8)
Christ The King Catholic Primary School, Bromborough

Iron The Super Rescuing Gecko

I have a gecko, his name is Iron
He is a very peculiar pet
He is not like a normal gecko but very cool instead
His scales are bright rainbow and he can walk on two legs
One night Iron was sleeping in his bed and he heard a cry
Iron the gecko please help me I am far too high
Iron the gecko put on his cape
He flew out of his tank and made a great escape
Iron found the baby gecko high in a tree
Oh dear baby gecko you are so high
Let me catch you
The baby gecko sprang out of the tree and *thump* onto iron knees
"Oof," said Iron as he tumbled to the ground
That baby gecko did a ground pound
The baby gecko was safe and Iron's job was done
Rescuing baby geckos is lots of fun.

Tessa Ashton-Martin (8)
Christ The King Catholic Primary School, Bromborough

Cheetawolf

C heetawolf gets up in the morning when it's time to wake me up in the morning.
H e always gets up to wake me up in the morning.
E ating cats, I have said no two times now, but you do it anyway!
E ven now, I love you, you're still naughty.
T he worst thing about him, he runs away to his comfy bed.
A lways running around like a lunatic!
W hat is wrong with my pet? He is such a lunatic.
O h no, he has run away! He is so fluffy.
L ove my pet, he's really fuzzy and faster than a cat.
F lying in the sky, just me and him.

Isabelle Johnson (8)
Christ The King Catholic Primary School, Bromborough

My Dog Called Dog

This is my dog
He's called Dog
He's my little baby boy
And he does not like the name Roy
If he sees a dog with one eye
He starts to cry
As the enormous blue tears fall down
He will start to howl
He also wears a bikini
He likes the character Luigi
He would love to fly
But he would never try
He is very sassy
He is also very classy
He is an amazing peculiar pet
He is more amazing than a dodo bird
He is as kind as a horse
He loves going upside down
Oh, he deserves a very large crown.
He wears an amazing hairstyle
But he would never wear a hat

His bikini is pink
Oh, what an amazing pick
He likes money
He's not being funny!

Max Jones (8)
Christ The King Catholic Primary School, Bromborough

The Tales Of The Chauocorn

There once was a man
Who was walking down an alleyway,
Suddenly, he heard a squeaking noise
Coming from a small cardboard box.
He lifted it up and had never be in such shock in his life
There it was
The Chauocorn.

The Chauocorn kept farting pink farts,
It ran around
Until it started shooting magic from its horn
And accidentally turned the man into a frog!
It bounced up and down
Not knowing what to do
The Chauocorn trotted off
Like nothing happened.

From now on
The Chauocorn lives out in the wild
And it now lives happily ever after
With many children and grandchildren.

Alfie Granton-Jones (10)
Christ The King Catholic Primary School, Bromborough

Eleeant

Eleeant is a funny, cool, little creature
And he loves his features.
He was going on a run
For some nice fun.
He saw something green
He felt like he was watching his friend Jean
But it was a bean!
Silly Eleeant got back from his run
And had to fill his tum.
Maybe crisps
With dips?
Eleeant loves food
Although he's a lazy dude
He sleeps on a twenty-foot-long bed
And he doesn't get fed
Eleeant said.
He loves a fake fight
But he gets a fright!
What a good day it has been

Oh no, he's been seen!
By the bean.
Oh, and it wasn't his friend Jean.

Lewis McWha (8)
Christ The King Catholic Primary School, Bromborough

The Dog And The Frog

Once, there was a dog
Who loved to run in the park
One day, he met a frog
And it made him bark

He barked that loud
It made the frog croak
The dog was convinced
The green frog was broke

The frog laughed at the dog
As he sat on a log
Because, even though it was dark,
The frog heard the dog fart!

They played all night
And had lots of fun
But the frog had a fright
When he fell, he hurt his bum

It was time for the dog to call it a day
He really needed to eat
They said goodbye, but before they left
They arranged their next meet.

LJ Black (11)

Christ The King Catholic Primary School, Bromborough

The Eight-Legged Giraffe James

James has breakfast in the morning
Then goes on a dark black motorbike quickly
Then he falls over.
James had a cut on his leg
He put a plaster on the cut.

He had some cheese sandwiches and salt and vinegar crisps
For lunch to get energy.
He had water for hydration
James felt better.

James is as slow as a slug
That is why he uses a black motorbike.
He is as stripy as a zebra
And as soft as a cat.

James is as tall as an elephant
As smooth as a dolphin.
James likes to play football and score
And has a wiggly, wormy tail.

Harry Stringer (8)
Christ The King Catholic Primary School, Bromborough

The Pretty Unidog

T he Unidog is always making everybody really happy.
H er horn is so glittery that it can make people's eyes shine.
E ating is one of her favourite things to do.

U nder the night sky, she looks at the beautiful dazzling stars.
N othing gets past her, she is amazing.
I took her on a walk and she sensed danger, so off she went...
D o all of you like my cute, adorable, stripy Unidog?
O n her birthday, she takes the day off to eat all the food, of course.
G o, go, go Unidog! Save the day, be a superhero.

Evie Wheadon (8)
Christ The King Catholic Primary School, Bromborough

My Aye-Aye In The Night

In the dead of night,
His large orange eyes shine bright.
When he gives you a stare,
It can give a scare,
My aye-aye in the night.

He has wiry hair,
His type is quite rare
He has a peculiar look
His long finger ready to hook
Onto fat wriggly grubs
That he hunts in the shrubs,
My aye-aye in the night.

I wish we could play
But he's asleep in the day
His long bushy tail
Ended up like the shell of a snail.
Some people say he's ugly
But I think he's lovely,
My aye-aye in the night.

Harry Forshaw (10)
Christ The King Catholic Primary School, Bromborough

The Gigantic And Gentle Dog

Whose dog is that?
I think I know.
Its owner is quite happy though.
Full of joy like a vivid rainbow.
I watch, laugh
I cry hello.
He gives his dog a shake
And laugh until his belly aches.
The only other sound's the break
Of distant waves and birds awake.
The dog is gigantic, gentle and deep
But he has promises to keep.
After cake and lots of sleep
Sweet dreams come to him cheap.
He rises from his gentle bed
With thoughts of kittens in his head.
He eats his jam with lots of bread
Ready for the day ahead.

Rosie Whiting (10)
Christ The King Catholic Primary School, Bromborough

Hippo Hero!

There was once a hippo
He was a real-life hero
He couldn't count past zero
His favourite actor was Robert De Niro.

He liked to play in the park
Which made the dogs bark
He always was afraid of the dark
And an angry shark

When he disobeyed the law
He never moved a paw
He saw an odd-looking door
That he went through once more

There he saw a marvellous Macaw
Who had two huge claws
He jumped upon the hippo
They danced together the Calypso

He is my very own hero!

Olivia Kitney (10)
Christ The King Catholic Primary School, Bromborough

Secret Predator

My cat is a secret predator
She hunts all through the night
The moon shines brightly upon her claws
Like a tiger big and bright.

She stalks the creatures slowly
Quietly, without a sound
She strikes like lightning upon her prey
Chasing them all around.

As the morning sun rises
She quickly returns home
She acts all cute and gentle
But nobody knows she went out to roam...

My cat is a secret predator
But I still love her so
Her name is Tattie, a rescue cat
So now you know!

Lily Strand (10)
Christ The King Catholic Primary School, Bromborough

My Greedy Cat

The other day, I found a cute fluffy cat.
It was miaowing a lot so I gave it a pat.
It was miaowing for food
I didn't know so it got in a mood.
Now I knew it was hungry, so it had food.
When I gave it food,
It dropped the mood
And the food on the floor!
As I looked over, I heard my door.
It was a strange man,
He had food in a pan.
The man gave me cat food as smelly as feet
The cat saw it, flavoured meat.
There wasn't a single miaow off the cat
I took care of it and gave it a pat.

Nicholas Horton (8)
Christ The King Catholic Primary School, Bromborough

Bob The Snail

B ob the snail is my pet, slimy and shiny.
O n the grass, coming towards me.
B ig and eating my strawberries and cabbage.

T en years old, loved the ice and hated the worms.
H e came to my house in the winter to see me.
E normous, he defends me and my house.

S limy, fast, a bit squashy he is.
N ativity he was in, now he is famous.
A unty Snail is here, yay!
I n school, he is on the chalkboard role.
L ily is his friend, kind and funny.

Isla Ann Moreau Heron (8)
Christ The King Catholic Primary School, Bromborough

Double Dog's Adventure

One day, I got a dog
He is not a normal dog
He is a dog with two heads
It can shoot red lasers out of its eyes
It can sprint super fast.

The good thing about my pet is
When I am in danger, he always saves me
Because he is as strong as a gorilla

On Monday, I went on a ride around our road
On Double Dog
All of the cars drove away
Because they were scared of my pet!

My pet is so fast
He accidentally ran into a lake.
We got home in a minute
That's how fast he is.

Michael Williamson (8)
Christ The King Catholic Primary School, Bromborough

The Charrat

T iny as a hamster, cute as a beautiful flower
H e is an amazing pet and furry and fluffy.
E ach mess he makes, he is very lazy.

C harming Charrat with spots and a beautiful face.
H e is colourful and a gentle cheetah parrot.
A fter he has done his lazy work, he daydreams.
R ight up and down he flies.
R ight work he does is beautiful
A nd he's charming with his beak which is dark.
T o his bed he goes and down again.

Lucas Jack Dack-Hughes (9)
Christ The King Catholic Primary School, Bromborough

Pet Called Noname

We have a peculiar pet,
We got him from the vet.

His breed is a mix of zebra and dog,
That is why he is called a Zebog.

His colours are black and also white,
To look at him would give you a fright.

He's furry and hairy,
In fact he's quite scary!

So I thought of a name, should we call it Joy?
Dad said, "You can't, because it's a boy."

So 11+ came and we got distracted,
He would have a name if only we'd acted...

Connor Duncan (10)
Christ The King Catholic Primary School, Bromborough

Spikey The Hedgehog

Have you ever seen a giant hedgehog?
I only saw it once on a walk,
I thought it was special,
So I ran home and got a dog lead,
It was small when I was taking it home,
It was tiny
But once I got home it was giant,
I had to let it sleep on my bedroom floor
In the morning, I had to ask him to shrink,
So I could put the lead on him
To take him on a walk,
He was speedy and I had to tell him, "Slow down,"
I kept him forever
Because he is the best pet ever.

Jake Daniel Formston (8)
Christ The King Catholic Primary School, Bromborough

Billionaire Marty And The Devil

Fifty miles from Saint Petersberg
Was a place called Dallol,
There lived a penguin called Marty,
He had a dog named Michael
Who was afraid of the fog
And as brown as a log.
They lived in a golden mansion
That glowed up at night.
Marty rode his bike
All around Dallol
And beeped at the Devil!
The Devil was planning to go to Oymyakon
But he had no money,
Michael felt bad for the Devil and gave him some money.
Then he can finally go to Oymyakon
Forever!

Harry Ethan Law (9)
Christ The King Catholic Primary School, Bromborough

Ginger The Whinger

My cat Ginger
Is a bit of a whinger.
After I'm back from school,
He's always miaowing.
Once, I came home from school
I decided to follow him.
He went to the kitchen and jumped onto the table.
He got the cake!
He ate it all up.
I thought he was very naughty.
He started dancing and partying,
Which was weird.
He partied like crazy.
He saw me watching him.
He came towards me and spoke.
He was angry,
It made him more of a ginger whinger!

Ruby Amelia Arrowsmith (8)
Christ The King Catholic Primary School, Bromborough

Rocky The Rockstar Dog

The other day, I adopted a dog,
He was small and cuddly and brown like a log
And every night, when the sun's gone down,
He grabs his guitar and begins to growl,
He thinks he's cool
But really he's a fool,
He's really loud
And tries to get a crowd
And when we go for walks,
He always talks
About his amazing rock-shock moves!
He loves chasing rabbits and eating carrots
And he's as dirty as a digger.
That's my amazing Rockstar Dog.

Grace Teese (9)
Christ The King Catholic Primary School, Bromborough

Rob The Rapper

When I came home from school,
I jumped into the pool.
I heard a cool dog
I couldn't see him at first
I thought he was a log
Because he blended in
But I knew he was a dog,
Who sat on a ragged log.
He jumps so high
And sparkles so bright like a star.
In the morning, he started to rap,
He also liked a pat.
Then he rapped down the road all day,
Then he said, "This is just like a game to play."
I called him Rob
And he sat on a log.

Manoa Masi (8)
Christ The King Catholic Primary School, Bromborough

Lazy Monkey

L azy is lying down on a flower bed
A t the zoo he demands kind zookeepers
Z ookeepers fall asleep as they watch Lazy
Y ellow beady eyes of his that you can't miss

M essy Lazy is always grumpy
O nly one person loves Lazy, that is himself
N ever has Lazy moved over
K een to demand his weekly sleep he broke the record
E ven his belly is as round as a football
Y ummy food he likes to eat, so yummy.

Anna Jarmulkowicz (8)
Christ The King Catholic Primary School, Bromborough

Fred The Crazy Dog

F reddy loves to ride his motorbike down the park.
R iding his motorbike, his trick just keeps on going with his fluffy fur.
E ating all the burgers that he sees.
D ragging his feet along the floor, he is so tired, it didn't hurt his little paws.

D own the hill, his motorbike ran out of charge!
O h my, he has gone so far!
G oing, running down the hill, he was running as fast as a cheetah as his ears were flapping.

Lara Michelle Cavanagh (8)
Christ The King Catholic Primary School, Bromborough

David The Racer

David is fast,
He goes in a flash,
David is as tall as a tree,
David, in his free time, goes to the mall
To get a spotty ball.
David loves speed,
And is bigger than a millipede.

His brother does F1 too,
They race together,
Forever and ever,
Three... two... one... go!
But David says, "Let them go first,
As the others will burst!
My car will stick to the ground,
I am bound
To win
And go past him..."

Seth Jones (8)
Christ The King Catholic Primary School, Bromborough

Cutey

My hamster is all rosy
She is very cute
She loves to eat
She likes to run on her wheel
She also likes to take a bath
She also likes to hang out with my family
She's small
She is cute and incredible
She loves to go behind our beds
She likes to wiggle like a worm
Sometimes she wiggles like a worm out of our hands!
She also likes to run away from us
She doesn't like loud noises
She doesn't like dogs lying with her.

Jacob Dack-Hughes (10)
Christ The King Catholic Primary School, Bromborough

Dinodog The Cheeky, Amazing, Crazy Dog

D inodog, cheeky, crazy dog.
I n the morning, he runs down the stairs, gets breakfast and goes to skate.
N o one is as good as him at skating.
O n Sunday, I took him out for a walk, he brought his skateboard and played.
D o you like my Dinodog? He is cute and playful.
O n the special day of the amazing competition of the dog final,
G o Dinodog! The cute, caring, amazing Dinodog won, yay! Well done, Dinodog.

Lucy Sawley (8)
Christ The King Catholic Primary School, Bromborough

Bunnycorn

B utterfly on her nose
U nicorn horn that is very magical
N ow she is playing hide-and-seek with her friends
N ow her friends find her under the big brown teddy
Y ou will love her so much
C ute when she is playing tea party with her unicorn teddy
O h, she is eating a pink pretzel
R ainbow glittering wings that shimmer in the beautiful night sky
N ow she is in bed with my phone.

Taylor Murphy (8)
Christ The King Catholic Primary School, Bromborough

Peculiar Pixy And Her New Glasses

Yesterday, I adopted a cat,
She was cute and cuddly and black like a bat.
But one thing that was strange, strange indeed,
She could not see at all.
So we went to the vets
And she had a rest.
Then she got some glasses,
They were as dark as a cave and like the night.
She was very strange, strange indeed,
So we called her Peculiar Pixy.
She may be strange but she is a delight,
A delight to live with, her and her glasses.

Mariola Kisiel (8)
Christ The King Catholic Primary School, Bromborough

Daisy The Cheeky Hamster

Have you ever seen a talking hamster?
I've seen one with my own eyes,
It asked what my name was,
It was very clever and cheeky and hungry,
It was big and fat after robbing every food place,
It had massive claws the size of a house,
She'd smash down the tall hard buildings
And it would eat, sleep and drink with its massive claws,
It would be funny when she fell,
She went away forever,
Never to be seen again.

Sean Verlander (9)

Christ The King Catholic Primary School, Bromborough

Royal The Peculiar Horse Girl

Royal is a very cute Gypsy Vanner horse
Royal loves Pepsi but hates clowns.
She loves dressage
She's never had a massage
She is pretty meek
And pretty sleek.
Royal is a dressage champ
She's *horse*-ome!
She hates hay
But loves the bay
Royal's very strange
She loves the Range!
Her favourite thing is black and white spotty socks.
She's pretty cold
Now she's getting old.

Rebecca Wood (8)
Christ The King Catholic Primary School, Bromborough

Darren The Dog

Have you ever seen a stray dog on the street?
I saw one on the street on the way home from school
It had a deadly bite and a beautiful sight
I gave it some steak
But it ran away, it needed a break
Soon the sun was setting
As wings grew out from its body
It flew away as it grew foggy
With its slimy wings
You could just about see it with its glowing wings
And it disappeared forever,
In the sky
Up high.

Daniel Carter (8)
Christ The King Catholic Primary School, Bromborough

Maria Duck

M inding her own business
A s she has her own money.
R eady for her favourite season soon.
I n the summer, she goes to the pond that she loves
A nd she has a husband.

D ucks love swimming but Maria Duck loves being rich.
U ses her umbrella every rainy day.
C uts her long gold curly hair every Sunday.
K ind of fancy day for Maria, in Paris.

Maggi Merrick (8)
Christ The King Catholic Primary School, Bromborough

Elegant Emma!

Once upon a time, there was a Rhinacorn
Woah, it had a triple horn!
Butterflies faint when she sings
Wow, she has rainbow wings!

Her tummy is as quiet as a mouse
Even when she saw a woodlouse
Her hooves are as bright as a light
They glow in the dark night.

I think she deserves a crown
Even when she's upside down
She has a wavy tail
She's as slow as a snail.

Aimee-Leigh Copeland (9)
Christ The King Catholic Primary School, Bromborough

Shankly The Goalkeeper Dog

Every day, when I come home from school,
My little puppy Shankly is sitting on the floor,
He is tall and skinny
With cute little brown eyes,
Running around crazy all the time,
Fast running out to get the ball,
We play all evening,
I try to give a fast, strong kick with the ball,
But Shankly is too good at being goalkeeper
We go in time to cuddle
On the couch until dinner.

Mia Loughnan (9)
Christ The King Catholic Primary School, Bromborough

My Pet Doggles

I have two dogs,
They like to play on logs,
They love going to the park
But they always bark,
One late starry night,
When it wasn't very bright,
They wouldn't run around,
They would just lie on the ground,
The grew shells and became Doggles,
They put on their goggles,
People say that makes them scary
But to me they are still family and still very furry!

Chloe Atkinson (10)
Christ The King Catholic Primary School, Bromborough

Angel

Angel is a dog
That looks like a log
She has no legs
She has no feet
She loves to eat
Her owner is a little girl
You know when she's coming
She goes thumping, thumping, thumping
Angel is very slow
She always comes last
Unlike Bess, who is very fast
Angel is a devil
Despite her sweet name
She isn't tame
Her mum always wanted to rename!

Gabrielle Jarmay (10)
Christ The King Catholic Primary School, Bromborough

Georgia The Giraffe Model!

Georgia the giraffe is very light
And sometimes she gets in a fight
Her dress is very tight
Be aware, sometimes she might bite

She has pink high heels
And because she's famous, she gets a good deal
She likes to get tickled
Once, she giggled
She likes to go in a limo
To Bongo's bingo
She has a long spotty tail
And her tail is really pale.

Georgia Edwards (8)
Christ The King Catholic Primary School, Bromborough

Jazz The Cat

I have never seen a cat that hates milk.
She couldn't jump that high
So I taught her.
I named her Jazz.
She gets hungry all the time
So I feed her toast.
She's always close to the kitchen
That's how I know she's hungry.
I let her play with me if she feels lonely.
Jazz is very cute and fluffy,
Just like a giant marshmallow.

Rosie Lorraine Martin (8)
Christ The King Catholic Primary School, Bromborough

My Owlet, My Friend

The other day, I helped an owl
She was stuck in a tree.
She was helpless, her wing was sprained
And she was in pain.
My mum is a vet,
She gave her a clean and check-up.
Have you ever helped a creature?
We played until Mum called us down for lunch.
I had fish fingers
Owlet had worms.
We played flying tag
We caught butterflies.

Maisie Thomson (8)
Christ The King Catholic Primary School, Bromborough

The Dashcorn

D ashing dog with magical powers.
A mazing power to heal others.
S hiny horn that shines in the night
H ide! The baddies are coming
C ourage as he fights the baddies
O h, his horn fell off!
R un! It's going to explode if it's not on his head
N ow we saved the day, all thanks to Dashcorn.

Charlotte Stout (10)
Christ The King Catholic Primary School, Bromborough

Bob My Snail

I had a pet called Bob the snail,
He was slow, fat and had a slimy tail.
It took him ages to cross the grass,
He climbed in a bottle
And was stuck in the glass.
One day, when the sun came out,
I shouted, "Bob, look out!"
In the blink of an eye,
I saw the moments we shared,
Before Bob was taken in the beak of a bird...

Michael Heron (10)
Christ The King Catholic Primary School, Bromborough

My Little Cutle

My little Cutle is fierce, fiery and brave,
Soft, cute and tiny,
He is as cute as a cupcake
But as mean as a tiger,
As slow as a snail and as fast as a cheetah!
My marvellous miniature pet has a shell with spots,
He has whiskers sprouting out of his loose skin,
There is nothing more I could ask for,
My little Cutle is just right!

Greta Gilchrist (10)
Christ The King Catholic Primary School, Bromborough

Lottey The Shy Turtle

Have you ever seen a turtle who can't swim?
I have only seen it once,
It looked like it could not swim,
It was small and cute
So I helped, but it was shy,
It got used to me,
It let me carry it out of the sea,
I fed it and helped it swim
And I let it go
To its family,
She swam off really quickly, fast,
Speedy.

Harlow Summer (8)
Christ The King Catholic Primary School, Bromborough

The Odd Buffalo

O dd Buf is different compared to other buffalos.
D oing what he likes is eating large lions.
D ancing around on his little five legs.

B uffalos were shocked because he was that odd.
U nderground Odd Buf lives, under the thick mud.
F lying, Odd Buf is off the ground, making the buffalos shocked.

Elijah Khozoie (8)
Christ The King Catholic Primary School, Bromborough

Jake The Dog

Jake is my peculiar pet,
He doesn't like to get his feet wet,
When going out in the rain,
You hear him complain
And he runs back in like a jet.

My dog can do some cool tricks,
He is good at collecting sticks,
He sniffs like a rabbit,
It's a really bad habit
But he gives lots of slobbery licks.

Olivia Quilliam (10)
Christ The King Catholic Primary School, Bromborough

The Woods With A Pet

I went for a walk in the woods last night
And saw a beast which gave me a fright
It looked at me with wild beady eyes,
Its dark red scales were a big surprise.
I opened my bag and took out my net,
I caught the beast and made him my pet!
He was grumpy, slimy, ferocious and spiny,
But, lucky for me, he was really tiny.

Daniel Pannell (10)
Christ The King Catholic Primary School, Bromborough

The Singing Unicat

U nicat was a champion, she was the greatest scooter driver ever.
N o one was better at driving a scooter than her.
I t is one of the greatest singers in the world.
C lever, chatty unicat.
A lways doing flips, flips on her scooter over walls.
T he Unicat loves to sing, eat and sleep.

Erin Cottrell (8)
Christ The King Catholic Primary School, Bromborough

Tilly The Telephant

Tilly the Telephant was just so elegant.
She was also as lazy as a daisy.
She was very tall and also noisy
She slept in her shell nice and cosy
She didn't like mice, they made her tremble
And if she could, she would hide under a table!
Tilly was as green as grass
As slow as a slug and shy like a mouse.

Ava Graves (10)
Christ The King Catholic Primary School, Bromborough

Prince The Smart Dog

Prince is a dog
But he loves being a frog!
He is cute and tall
But he would rather be small.
Prince is smart
And likes his art.
Drawing, drawing until the morning.
Football-mad Prince can take a free kick
But when he misses,
He has to do the dishes!
Dear Prince,
You are my best friend.

Luca Porter (8)
Christ The King Catholic Primary School, Bromborough

The Great Frog Gordo

My frog jumps and plays.
My frog always jumps away.
He jumps and flies
He catches flies.
He falls and he doesn't cry.
He has super strength
And goes into a long length.
He's crazy, he went to the moon
On my trampoline to the moon
He saw a cow and a spoon
Flying over the moon!

Luka Thomas (8)
Christ The King Catholic Primary School, Bromborough

Mr Bark's Day!

Mr Bark
Went to the park,
He ate some bark
And played in the dark,
Then he made a friend called Mark.
They went home
Went in the back and played with the foam,
Then they went on a trip to Rome
And found a gnome!
Then they went on Google Chrome
And found another friend called Jerome.

Samuel Jones (10)
Christ The King Catholic Primary School, Bromborough

Wonky Donkey

We had a donkey,
We named her Wonky,
Wonky is a fatty,
She's also an Insta baddy!
Big lips,
Medium hips,
She's always tripping,
Her lipgloss is always dripping,
She's always wearing make-up,
But her face looks like it blew up!
It began to rain,
Wonky Donkey lost fame.

Layla Higham (10)
Christ The King Catholic Primary School, Bromborough

An Old Cat

There was an old cat
Who was part bat
And had a very, very long tail.
The extraordinary beast
Had a feast
His eyes as thin as a veil.
This peculiar thing
Flew with bat wings
As black as the midnight sky.
Flying to the edge of the atmosphere
This cat bat definitely had no fear!

Alfie Drury (10)
Christ The King Catholic Primary School, Bromborough

Crazy Cat

C razy cat Cuddles likes to jump in puddles.
U nique in every way.
D elightful, he chases mice.
D ashing and dancing along the way.
L icking his ice lolly on a hot day.
E ating lots of chocolate cake.
S leeps on his mat as he dreams about his day.

Amelia Jane Hughes (8)
Christ The King Catholic Primary School, Bromborough

The Odd Boys

Fred was a cat-faced sausage dog with chicken wings!
He was owned by a man called Greg.
You could say that Greg was a shy guy
Who always stayed in the corner
Because he felt like he didn't fit in!
And in a way
You could say
That Fred was the same
But just an animal!

Olivia Murphy (10)
Christ The King Catholic Primary School, Bromborough

Gorita's Personality List

G orita is a marvellous pet to have.
O ccasionally ferocious but mainly he is messy.
R idiculously furry in all body parts.
I ntelligently wise so he makes me smart.
T ogether we make the most ferocious team.
A lways makes my bad dreams disappear.

Lewis Beacall (11)
Christ The King Catholic Primary School, Bromborough

Tale About A Snail

There was a snail called Slumpy
He could be a little grumpy
When the ground was lumpy
He grew as big as a whale
He was scared to fail
He wished he was gentle
But he was just a bit mental!
He thought he was classy
But he was just sassy
Feeling trashy.

Ava Gadsby (10)
Christ The King Catholic Primary School, Bromborough

Super Spud

S mall
U nusual
P otato by another name.
E njoys flying
R olls quickly

S aving people in danger is his aim
P opular and famous.
U nforgettable.
D efinitely the best pet in the world!

Jack Herbert (8)
Christ The King Catholic Primary School, Bromborough

Buffmiester

Four legs,
Scratchy bum,
Soft and fluffy,
I wonder what this peculiar pet could be,
A dog that's a girl
And she's a troublemaker, reminds me of me,
If she chases her tail, she'd swirl
And she lies on the sofa, watching TV.

Chloe Issabella Dixon (10)
Christ The King Catholic Primary School, Bromborough

Tortoises Are Actually Fast

I had a little tortoise
Very quick and fast
And in a race, always
Never last.
She could not be surpassed!
Along the track she went
It seemed so long and vast
But then and there I saw it
She would never
Be last.

Ben Hughes (10)

Christ The King Catholic Primary School, Bromborough

The Slothasaurus

I am a Slothasaurus, I am unique,
It is unlikely that we will meet,
I am endangered and very rare,
No other animals can compare,
I am great just how I am,
I love me for being me
And that's what I hope you can see.

Emily Mosedale (10)
Christ The King Catholic Primary School, Bromborough

Stuart The Snerd

S tuart the Snerd is a marvellous pet
N ight-time is his playtime
E ight legs he has, he likes
R aces because he beats everyone, but
D aylight he turns back into a snake.

Curtis McAloon (10)
Christ The King Catholic Primary School, Bromborough

Maisy

Maisy is Grandad's dog
It's small and white
I go round to see her
She wiggles her tail and licks my hand
When I leave, I wish I could take her with me
But she is Grandad's dog.

Sophie Bradley (10)
Christ The King Catholic Primary School, Bromborough

Coco The Cockatoo

I have a cockatoo
She likes to wear one shoe
She's white and fluffy,
With big blue eyes
And her beak is quite pointy too.

Emily Richards (10)
Christ The King Catholic Primary School, Bromborough

Zelda

My pet Zelda is an Arctic fox,
It's white and fluffy with lots of specks,
She is sweet and fluffy and absolutely
extraordinary,
That's my Zelda, an Arctic fox.

My pet Zelda is a winter pine marten,
It's tiny, white and furry with turquoise, purple and
pink dots,
She is tiny, agile and friendly,
That's my Zelda, a winter pine marten.

My pet Zelda is a large flying dragon,
It's large, scaly and loyal,
She is a good fighter but also very friendly,
That's my Zelda, a large flying dragon.

My pet Zelda is a small glowing snow spider,
It's tiny, blue, with a gleaming body,
She is tiny, feisty and can hide in my pocket,
That's my shape-shifting Arctic fox, Zelda.

Rosie Studdy (10)
Rawcliffe Primary School, Rawcliffe

My Magical Guinea Pigs

My guinea pigs are magical,
They're brown and white, ginger and black,
They adore fruit and veg,
But magical apples are the best,
Bubble and Squeak, Bubble and Squeak,
My pet guinea pigs Bubble and Squeak.

My guinea pigs are magical,
They can speak and squeak their spells out loud,
They wear glasses all around.
Bubble and Squeak, Bubble and Squeak,
My pet guinea pigs Bubble and Squeak.

My guinea pigs are magical,
The Arctic is their home,
They live in a lovely ice dome
Bubble and Squeak, Bubble and Squeak,
My pet guinea pigs Bubble and Squeak.

My guinea pigs are magical,
They're sassy with their words
But if you don't annoy them, I promise they won't hurt.
Bubble and Squeak, Bubble and Squeak,
My guinea pigs Bubble and Squeak.

Holly Lane (10)
Rawcliffe Primary School, Rawcliffe

Pob The Cob

There was a horse named Pob
Who was a black and white cob
And every year she did the horse job
Which was competing in a race
She always had to face
Sophie and her horse case
That's not it
There's Lilly and Mit

Pob's owner is called Leah
Who has an evil friend called Mia
And she is competing with her horse Jet
The fastest yet!
And was last year's winner
Pob got ready for the show after her dinner

When she arrived
It was a maze to her eyes
Pob itched her nervous fur
She wouldn't let that stop her
And they were off
But Leah had a cough

Ten minutes later the race was done
With a cheer, Pob and Leah won!
To celebrate they shared a bun.

Annie Hollingsworth (9)
Rawcliffe Primary School, Rawcliffe

Tim The Turtle

I have a turtle and his name is Tim
He likes to eat
But he cannot swim
He can dance when he's in the mood
He also likes to try a lot of food
He can be a little eccentric
But keep him away from water because he is electric!
One day, there was an awful pong
I chucked him in the bath and wondered what was wrong
His head went *pop!* and his shell went *bang!*
Tim was dead and an ambulance we rang
That was the end of Tim the electric turtle
I took the blame and that was very hurtful
So we all got in a circle
And prayed for Tim the electric turtle.

Tommy Rooke (9)
Rawcliffe Primary School, Rawcliffe

Gwen The Fire-Breathing Chicken

I used to have a chicken and its name was Gwen.
I bought it because I thought it was an egg-laying hen.
One day, I went to check the coop to see if she had laid,
My eyes were shocked to look and find the mess she had made!
The hay was burnt to cinders and the coop was gone,
I turned around to find poor Gwen and asked her what was wrong.
Her mouth was fully open and smoke filled the sky
And that was when a fireball flew straight at my eye!
Now I have no chicken or laying hen,
But I have a chicken dragon and her name is Gwen.

Louis Bean (11)
Rawcliffe Primary School, Rawcliffe

Tony The Flexible Tiger

There once was a tiger named Tony
He didn't like to eat food that was bony
Most of the time he was thrilled
He also was properly skilled
All his circus friends were rude
So he was always in a mood
He never liked being in the circus
'Cause everyone said he was worthless!
One day, the tiger had snapped
All of his friends clapped
Tony was so flexible
He always liked eating his vegetables
He doesn't like seeing a fox
But likes playing with his best friend Moss.

Tamzin Pearse-Drury (11)
Rawcliffe Primary School, Rawcliffe

My Carnivorous Pets

As the sun comes up on another day
The carnivorous plants await their prey
They're sticky, slimy and even a little snappy
Who will they eat today?

Releasing their delicious scents
Which little creature will take the bait?
There the plants will wait

Pitchers ready
Jaws wide open
A shiny dewdrop glistening in the sun
Who will they eat today?

With a sticky encounter
A deadly snap
A deep dark pitcher
There is no turning back!

Archie Harding (10)
Rawcliffe Primary School, Rawcliffe

Candyfloss

Candyfloss, Candyfloss my pet kitten,
Soft and snuggly like a mitten,
Fluffy, adorable but very smitten,
That's my Candyfloss, my pet kitten.

Candyloss, Candyfloss my pet kitten,
She carries joke cards wherever she goes,
But she doesn't like it when it snows,
That's my Candyfloss, my pet kitten.

Candyfloss, Candyfloss my pet kitten,
She lives in the clouds
In a lovely candy house,
That's my Candyfloss, my pet kitten.

Elle-May Clough (10)
Rawcliffe Primary School, Rawcliffe

Blueberry The Flying Narwhal

Blueberry loves to swim around
In the pink glittery sea,
All the fishes give her kisses
And dream about what they could be.
Blueberry is deep blue with splats
of light blue too,
She uses her pink glittery horn for magic
But don't worry, only good spells are coming for
you.
Blueberry likes to eat Oreos and doughnuts,
She uses her feathery wings to fly around
the world how cool,
I'd like to travel with her
What about you.

Keida Krawciw (9)
Rawcliffe Primary School, Rawcliffe

My Magic

Street Magic,
That's tragic,
And all his fish are pelagic.
Did you see his fire?
Don't be a liar
Or you will get a flaming tyre.
Vimto fizzy makes him dizzy
And Magic's kinda tizzy.
I found him on the street,
He was walking with bare feet,
So I tucked him under my sheet.
Magic died,
Everyone blamed me and cried,
I was horrified!
Magic, rest in peace,
Now his sheet has no crease.

Zail Morrell (10)
Rawcliffe Primary School, Rawcliffe

A Kitten Called Mitten

I once had a kitten
Called Mitten
He lived in Great Britain
Instead of flittin',
He'll be sittin'.
Next to her, I'm cheerful and smitten

He was just a kitten
Always playing with my mittens
He's covered in fur
The noise he makes is a wonderful purr
When asleep, he curls into a ball
Which makes him look very small
That's why I was smitten
By my kitten.

Ashley Ward (9)
Rawcliffe Primary School, Rawcliffe

Alexa The Elephant

Alexa the elephant
Alexa the elephant
When she performs
She transforms
Alexa the elephant
When she walks on the wire
She falls into the fire
Alexa the elephant
Every day she performs in the circus
But she thinks she is worthless
She gets in a strop when things go wrong
Because everyone is gone
She always performs
But only once more
Alexa, Alexa
Poor Alexa.

Harriet Stanger (10)
Rawcliffe Primary School, Rawcliffe

Leafy The Ruler

Leafy the ruler
Is cooler than most rulers.
He flies in the sky
And sees birds passing by.
Leafy loves apples,
To get them down he uses a grapple
And he likes to pray in a chapel.

He likes to get his favourite bottle
And if he doesn't get home in time, he'll get a throttle!
Leafy the ruler's parents are lazy
But soon they'll be able to grow a bunch of daisies.

Jayden Joy (10)
Rawcliffe Primary School, Rawcliffe

Hedgie My Flying Hedgehog

Hedgie, my flying hedgehog,
Fast, cuddly and cute,
Purple spikes, fast in flight,
Hedgie, my happy hedgehog.

Hedgie, my flying hedgehog,
Always eating all day,
Blueberries, nuts and strawberries,
Hedgie, my happy hedgehog.

Hedgie, my flying hedgehog,
Flying forward and back,
Hovering inches off the ground,
Hedgie, my happy hedgehog.

Gabriella Hermann (10)
Rawcliffe Primary School, Rawcliffe

A Lion That Lies

There was a lion that always told lies,
No matter how much he tries,
He always tells lies,
No one likes the lion that lies
And he always cries,
He lives alone
Chewing on his bone,
No one rings his phone,
He is all alone,
The lion is a pie maker,
He is a super baker,
No one comes to share his pies
Because he is the lion that tells lies.

Chloe Barker (10)
Rawcliffe Primary School, Rawcliffe

The Sausage Dog

The small sausage dog
Met a big fat frog
Whose name was Clog
Who sat on an uncomfortable log.

The small flying sausage
Was called Flying Saucer,
Flying Saucer was very high
In the sky.
From the corner of his eye
He saw Clog the frog
Jumping high from his log.

Before you knew it,
The dog and frog were best friends.

Connie Holt (9)
Rawcliffe Primary School, Rawcliffe

Flying Cat That Talks

I thought to go on a walk
But then I heard someone talk
It was a cat wearing a clock
It came as a shock
I started crying
Surprisingly, the cat started flying
The cat called my name
I thought I was going insane
He told me not to be afraid
So next to the cat I did lie
We became the best of friends
And that's how the story ends.

Lilly Jackson (10)
Rawcliffe Primary School, Rawcliffe

Deygu, Deygu

Deygu, Deygu
You have big ears and long tails
Even though they are sharp,
You never scratch me with your nails.

Deygu, Deygu
One of you is brown, the other is white
You play all day
And sleep all night

Deygu, Deygu
You climb on my back
You love your food
And you climb like a cat.

Theo Wood (9)
Rawcliffe Primary School, Rawcliffe

This Is No Ordinary Dog

This is no ordinary dog,
he lives in a log.
Because he is so long,
but something is wrong.

This is no ordinary dog,
his friend is a frog.
He is sad,
and also really mad.

This is no ordinary dog,
he cannot jog.
He sees a hog,
so he hides in the log!

Jake Gutteridge (10)
Rawcliffe Primary School, Rawcliffe

Autumn Tiger

Tame as a house cat
Wild as a dragon

Her coat is like autumn
Mingling with the trees

Velvet paws on wet grass
Her voice sounding like a gang

Glaring suspiciously at the leaves
Carefully watching...

Harry Loombe (9)
Rawcliffe Primary School, Rawcliffe

Mitten The Kitten

I once had a kitten
Called Mitten
Who lives in Great Britain.
My kitten is funny
And played with a bunny.
That's why he lives in Great Britain.

Marley Shakespeare (9)
Rawcliffe Primary School, Rawcliffe

The Lonely Penguin

I'm a little penguin in the North Pole
I slide on my tummy to get cold
I splash in water and other places too
I have friends that do the same too!

Amelia Bussey (9)
Rawcliffe Primary School, Rawcliffe

My Cow

I never saw a more funny cow
It is really good at milking
It is not a cow that says, "Pow,"
And she can't help smirking!

Tymo Dickinson (9)
Rawcliffe Primary School, Rawcliffe

My Penguin King

My penguin is a king,
He dances with his Ling
He eats gold,
Talks to Nold
And plays ping-pong with Ling

Edmund Wilson (9)
Rawcliffe Primary School, Rawcliffe

Hungry

A haiku

A great monster dog,
Skeleton legs, twenty tongues,
Five times as hungry!

Robert Broderick (11)

Rawcliffe Primary School, Rawcliffe

Lilly The Flying Giraffe

L illy the flying giraffe is as fast as an eagle.
I n the night and the day she's flying unseen.
L illy is my pet, she's rare all around.
L illy makes me happy when we go on lots of rides.
Y ip, yap, yay, we fly night and day.

T he wind in my face is really ace.
H er neck is really furry.
E lephants look so short when we're flying through the blue.

F lying above gardens and houses too.
L ike a swooping eagle, but bigger than a cow, she's flying, but how?
Y ip, yap, yay, we fly night and day.
I n the moonlight we swoop down low.
N ibbling apples and carrots.
G ardens are the size of a pin.

G ood fun in the sky.
I t's a nice day to be out.
R oaring through the sky, it's amazing how we fly.
A nd all the trees are tiny.
F inished outside,
F or the clouds we ride.
E ndless fun too when we eat a bun.

Dylan Cox (8)

Sebert Wood Community Primary School, Bury St Edmunds

Ajetic Snakasaurus

A jetic Snakasaurus is speeding through space.
J ets are way slower than his jetpack.
E xtremely weird and cool scales.
T hick and very colourful scales.
I cy eyes.
C ameras spying in space on his jetpack.

S nakes following everywhere he goes.
N ick is his first name.
A s he flies through galaxies, he sees aliens.
Catches up to everyone in a race.
K ites are his worst nightmare.
A t his house, it's all sticky.
S ocks are clothes for him
A dventure is his middle name
U sually he kills lizards.
R ocks are stuck on the bottom of him.
U n is his favourite number
S ky is his last name.

Luke Frias (8)
Sebert Wood Community Primary School, Bury St Edmunds

Super Scaly Snake

S uper Scaly Snake eating cake
U pon the hay, to the park, you make me laugh
P ushing me on the swings, doing his snake thing
E very day when we walk home, we will fly a drone
R uining everything in his path

S o epic when you are flying to save the day
C aring for others
A n epic lifesaver, stronger than anything
L ikes going crazy in a battle
Y ou're saving the universe

S uper Scaly Snake always back in time for tea
N ever-ending centuries you have been fighting forever
A t our home, making a dome
K ing of snakes in your dome, all you do is roam
E verybody worship the Super Scaly Snake.

Henry Jenkins (9)
Sebert Wood Community Primary School, Bury St Edmunds

Snakapede

S wimming in the lake at night, my Snakapede might give you a fright
N ever fear, he is friendly if you go near
A desert-dweller usually, I brought him back to live with me
K eep feeding him pickles, grass and leaves, he's really not that hard to please
A thousand legs crawling along, with him is where I belong
P lenty of games that we can play, you can join if you say hey
E xoskeleton climbing trees, careful not to fall from the breeze
D iving around in the garden as soon as those skies darken
E nd of the night we fall into our beds, listen carefully, you may hear our zeds.

Arthur Wallis (8)
Sebert Wood Community Primary School, Bury St Edmunds

The Gecko

There, from the corner of my eye,
I saw a gecko, I looked at its tail
And it looked spotty and pale.

I looked at its sharp claws
They looked like fluffy paws.
In the gecko's mouth, I stared at a bright pink flower
That was as tall as a tower.

I named it Mango
Because it was cute and then it started doing the Tango.

I watched the gecko's eyes
I saw they were bright yellow
And I thought he said, "Hello."

He had colourful spots
That looked like dazzling dots.
His house was made of firewood
That stood very good.

Ashkan Talebpour (8)
Sebert Wood Community Primary School, Bury St Edmunds

Little Bob

Me and my dog
Really, really love to rob
Today we've got a plan
To steal a ring from Uncle Sam.
Me and my dog loved to run
And besides, it was all fun.
As we got to the door
The dog cut it open with a saw.
As we ran in
I caught a glimpse of the ring
As we ran in the room
I realised it was just a spoon!
I tiptoed back
Sly as a cat
Then we saw an old man in bed
With the ring strapped to his head
I slapped the old man in his bed
And stole the ring from his head
I passed it down to my dog
"Oh yeah!" His name is Little Bob.

Charlie Boughton (8)
Sebert Wood Community Primary School, Bury St Edmunds

Doom Danger Dog

Doom Danger Dog had a very whacky wound.
Doom Danger Dog is as green as glass.
Doom Danger Dog has eyes as bright as an angel singing on the darkest night.
Doom Danger Dog is too cute to resist.
Doom Danger Dog is as grumpy as a lion.
Doom Danger Dog loves dog food.
Doom Danger Dog is too sticky to stop.
Doom Danger Dog brings danger and is a rager!
Doom Danger Dog loves the clock but hates the tick-tock.
Doom Danger Dog loves the phone but hates the tone.
Doom Danger Dog is very fond of the big main pond.

Jayden Mcanally (8)
Sebert Wood Community Primary School, Bury St Edmunds

Ajetic Cat

A jetic Cat flies towards the rusty mat.
J umping around on the grey dirty ground.
E xtremely slimy and grimy floor.
T hick jetpack which makes a lightning burst.
"I am as quick as a light."
C ameras trying to attack Cat, but Ajetic Cat is too quick.

C at catches up with everyone.
A s Cat flies in the house, he finds some yummy pies.
T he cat flies out of the house and finds cupcakes on the ground.

Daniel Atanasov (8)
Sebert Wood Community Primary School, Bury St Edmunds

Tilly And The Tigerphant

"Hello, my name is Tilly, I have a Tigerphant.
She is as soft as a panda but as fierce as a lion."
Her anger is as hot as an iron!

I sometimes sit on her back,
Carrying a flour sack,
Her tail swishes and swashes along the rail.
I tie hay bales
While carrying the sack.

I clean her tusk
At dusk.
She adores her stripes
While I ride my bike.

I cuddle up next to her
Just after supper.

Aaliyah Ali (9)
Sebert Wood Community Primary School, Bury St Edmunds

Ten Things Found In A Plasamoure's Belly

A smelly, stinky carcas.
A small Plesamoure's egg.
A bone the size of a stone.
A person as old as the moon.
A pair of glasses that he wears.
A book that he reads when he has got his glasses on.
A radio that he listens to when he is bored.
A pair of hearing aids, he wears them when he talks to his friends so he can hear them.
A fluffy duster that the old man tickles him with.
A class of kids he annoyed!

Charlie Bugg (9)
Sebert Wood Community Primary School, Bury St Edmunds

Catsnake

C arefully and quietly he carried his food
A nxiously he thought about being discovered
T rees are his favourite and he lives in them
S uspiciously he heard a human voice
N oisily the humans talked about discovering a new species
A ll of a sudden the voices got quieter
K icking through the leaves, the humans walked away
E xcellent, thought the smart, scary catsnake.

Hugo Spurling (8)
Sebert Wood Community Primary School, Bury St Edmunds

Buttersaur

B uttersaur
U nique wings as bright as gold and as big as an elephant.
T iny legs as slim as a pencil and as messy as a pig.
T errifying claws that could kill a human.
E xtraordinary nest the size of a car park.
R aised neck as graceful as a ballerina.
S uper flyer, watch him go.
A mazing at running.
U FO driver in his spare time.
R oar!

Theo Mitcham (8)
Sebert Wood Community Primary School, Bury St Edmunds

Kittycorn

K ites fly in the air with gentle winds.
"I love to fly!"
T iny cars on the smooth ground.
T he total of blue houses is 10,000!
"Y ou are ready to go to the amazing air."
C orn is the favourite food for yellow Kittycorns.
O h my, what a colourful rainbow!
R ats hate pink Kittycorns!
N o one grumpy, everyone is happy!

Anita Bozhkova (8)
Sebert Wood Community Primary School, Bury St Edmunds

Pig Pop Pig

P ig Pop Pig ate a pie
"I ate chocolate chip ice cream!" said Pig Pop Pig.
G iggles gave Pig Pop Pig hiccups

P ig Pop Pig loves ice cream
O h dear, he got muddy jumping in a
P uddle. *Splash!*

P ig Pop Pig saw a small leaf.
"I love food."
"G rr!" Oh Pig Pop Pig, you're hungry.

Bella Young (8)
Sebert Wood Community Primary School, Bury St Edmunds

The Day We Saw A Mammoth

As me and my Huphoenix were flying down a street,
We saw a mammoth with seven feet.
My Huphoenix grabbed it with its claws
And we flew straight to a horse.
When we were above the horse,
My Huphoenix dropped the mammoth on the floor.
The horse was kind but as violent as a demon.
Me and my bright, beautiful Huphoenix flew back to our house
Then we went to sleep.

Katya Sytnik (8)
Sebert Wood Community Primary School, Bury St Edmunds

Heroic Henry The Super Cat

As I go flying next to my super cat Heroic Henry
We glide as gracefully as a bird.
His super sight spies danger.
We swoop down to see a woman dangling from a cliff.
We knew we had to help her.
When we got her to safety, she was overjoyed.
"You saved my life!" she said
We flew off to help again
"Our work is never done!"

Emily Blackwell (9)
Sebert Wood Community Primary School, Bury St Edmunds

Bertie The Spy Cat

Bertie was a fluffy kitten
Her fur was as soft as a mitten
One day, she found out she was a spy
Her owner shouted, "My oh my!"
She was a fabulous spy cat
With support from her owner Matt
She can solve so many clues
It is so hard for her to lose
She is on a winning strike
In the basket of Matt's bike.

Evie Merton (8)
Sebert Wood Community Primary School, Bury St Edmunds

Ten Things Found In An Elly-Ant's Pocket

Picnic food as big as a human
A whole jar of water with no lid
An ant house with no one in it
A lake full of fish
A boy ant that is brown
A banana that is rotten
A trunk as big as an elephant
A car as small as a piece of grass
A dictionary that doesn't tell you anything.
A carrot that has a hole in it.

Ellis Chetcuti (8)
Sebert Wood Community Primary School, Bury St Edmunds

My Pet Robotic Kippo

R ad.
O mnivore.
B est.
O ne who is as awesome as Iron Man.
T eeth as sharp as iron nails.
I nvincible!
C ool.

K eagan's pet
I ndestructible
P roperly good at video games.
P erfect
O nly Robotic Kippo!

Keagan Heflin (8)
Sebert Wood Community Primary School, Bury St Edmunds

Ninja Cat

N ice
I mpressive
N imble
J ovial
A wesome

C urious
A nnoying
T enacious.

Sonny Hooper (8)
Sebert Wood Community Primary School, Bury St Edmunds

Steve

Steve is a fashionable pig.
He wears flashy shirts, glasses and a wig.
He went to town
To buy a new gown,
Then danced with a funky earwig!

Freddy Shore (8)
Sebert Wood Community Primary School, Bury St Edmunds

Cheeky The Peculiar Pet

P eculiar pets are amusing.
E ach animal is different.
C heeky likes to eat flies and bananas.
U nusual animals are always around us.
L ittle or large.
I rregular shapes and sizes.
A rtistic are some.
R ealistic or not.

P ets need walking every day.
E xtra food is also needed.
T raining is essential.
S leep and blankets are required to make a
happy pet.

Daisy Tilley (8)
St Bernadette's Catholic Primary School, Birmingham

Clever KAT

KAT is clever,
No one has beaten her, never,
She is smart
And has a kind heart
And she also likes jam tarts,
Sometimes mischievous,
But not the greediest,
She is a cat that can fly
And don't ask why.
She has a flower hat
And a coloured mat,
She is so cute,
But also minute.
KAT is rainbow-coloured,
Never gets a word wrong,
That is all I've heard.

Joyce Biniam (8)
St Bernadette's Catholic Primary School, Birmingham

Lacy The Dancer

L acy, a person? No, a Lamma
A no-common Lamma
C olourful but funny
Y ou will laugh for a year

D ancing like a diva
A s if she is dreaming
N ice like a tiger
C ute like she is from a different planet, ever so sweet
I like her lovely fur
N asty to bad people
G iving people kisses.

Abigail Bovas (9)
St Bernadette's Catholic Primary School, Birmingham

Muesa And Medusa

Hi, I am Muesa
I just eat
I have a sister
Her name is Medusa
She hardly eats.
Me and Medusa always fight
Me and Medusa have favourite owners!
The person who bought us is Medusa's favourite owner
And my favourite owner is her son, Uzayr.
I hardly ever purr
Medusa purrs a lot!
Medusa probably loves everyone!
Me and Medusa have play balls.

Zunariah (8)
St Bernadette's Catholic Primary School, Birmingham

Ballet Bonny

B akes cakes before I go
A dorable bunny
L azy pet
L ovely dancer
E xtraordinary, sweet
T iny pet

B eautiful ballerina
O pportunity to win
N ice costume
N ew dance shoes
Y ummy snack before she goes on stage.

Lexie Walsh (8)
St Bernadette's Catholic Primary School, Birmingham

Shelly

My name is Shelly
I love blue dairy
Like no other turtle
My scales are shiny
My scales are soft like sheep's fur
Like no other turtle
I run as fast as the wind
I love people
And they love me
I watch Pee Wee in the night
I am a Ninja Turtle
And I love pop!

Alfie Russell (9)
St Bernadette's Catholic Primary School, Birmingham

Doman

Doman, why do you run like that?
Doman, why do you have a funny hat?
Doman, you lovely cat.
Doman, who named you so odd?
Doman, why do you sing like that?
Doman, why do you dance like that?
Doman, you love the sea and tea!

Kelvin Mutebi Wamala (8)
St Bernadette's Catholic Primary School, Birmingham

Turtle Cat

Turtle Cat
You can be found in my hat
His favourite place to be is in the sea
That is the place we meet for tea

Turtle Cat
Is so fat
He can't fit in his shell
Good thing as it does smell!

Harrison Plant (9)

St Bernadette's Catholic Primary School, Birmingham

Model Dog

M essy pooch
O range and blue
D angerous sometimes
E xtraordinary beauty
L azy

D efinitely a dog
O n the bed all day
G entle sometimes.

Cassie-Jo Smith-Silver (8)
St Bernadette's Catholic Primary School, Birmingham

Chex

I am a wonderful creature
From far, far away.
I like fun adventures
They're more than one way
I'm fluffy and spotty
My tail is insane
You think I am pretty

Guess who I am?

Greta Raubiska (8)
St Bernadette's Catholic Primary School, Birmingham

Catybatsnake

A cat
And a bat
We can't find her
She's really kind
She's really sneaky but kind
I still can't find her
She's a bat
And a cat
She loves tea
And the sea.

Sophie Bromage (8)
St Bernadette's Catholic Primary School, Birmingham

Peculiar Pet

There was a grumpy snail
He got worrying mail
Telling him that he had to go to jail!
He started to pack his laser
But they told him to pack his razor...

Connor Watkins (8)
St Bernadette's Catholic Primary School, Birmingham

Lovely Lala

Lovely Lala
Loves being cute
Her favourite game is to play together
She loves being pretty
She is a real cutie
And she's my best friend too.

Adeena Anjum (8)
St Bernadette's Catholic Primary School, Birmingham

D J Zigy

D oing raps
J oining dancing

Z igging about
I t loves eating
G oing crazy
Y es, out!

Isam Malik (8)
St Bernadette's Catholic Primary School, Birmingham

My Robot Dog Electric Robby

Electric Robby
Devious and sneaky-ious.
Electric Robby
Stands proud and loud.
Electric Robby
I sure love this Bobby!

Jersey Kinnelly (8)
St Bernadette's Catholic Primary School, Birmingham

Skateboarding Cool Cat

F urry Funny Ball is growing really tall
U sing a jetpack that looks like a backpack
R unning to the competition hall that is really cool
R ustling his fur so much that it's a blur
Y ou will shout when he enters the hall.

F urry Funny Ball is looking like a bunny
U sing his farts to fly into the hall
N ot like normal farts, it smells like candy
N ot even a second late!
Y our face will brighten up all day

B ins are everywhere, full of snakes,
A ll the people are cheering like mad
L astly, he does the triple loop-the-loop
L astly, he screeches to a halt.

Jayden Wong (8)
Swaffham Bulbeck CE Primary School, Swaffham Bulbeck

Cutiepet

C utiepet, what do you eat? "I eat cat food like a cat."
U mbrellas fly sky high and dive like a beautiful swan
T oday, what will I do? "I will eat some crisps and go to bed."
I f you challenge my pet it will cheat like a cheetah
E verywhere he goes he flies with his scooter
P eculiar pets, why are you peculiar? Is it because you're weird or because you're funny?
E ats too much to get a big tummy
T ime is valuable, you know why? Because if time runs out on me I'll tell my mother, "Please can I have more time?" That's the proper thing to do.

Tanaka Mafuva (7)
Swaffham Bulbeck CE Primary School, Swaffham Bulbeck

The Secret Insect Spy

Rogina was a spy stick insect.
She liked solving crimes.
Rogina has policeman friends
And her favourite food is limes.
She uses a doll's car to get around.
She is in a shop, camouflaged to thyme.
She really needs a pound coin to buy a bag of limes.
When she went out the shop, her shirt tore.
She went back in the shop
And got a piece of material to tie to her waist.
She saw an apple and nibbled on it
Till she could see the core.
She was so fat now
A crowd of people gathered round
So she decided to bow.
Then she showed off her spy stuff
Her moves with her net, cameras and grapple hook.

Sophie Blundell (8)
Swaffham Bulbeck CE Primary School, Swaffham Bulbeck

Puppsie Puppsie

P uppsie,
U nhappy
P uppsie,
P aw
S aid
"I
E njoy

T urnips with
H am,
E ven

P arsnips
U nder the chair."
P uppsie
P uppsie
S aid
"I
E njoy

D igging
O nions,
G lorious onions!"

Puppsie Puppsie likes to dance in the moonlight.
Puppsie Puppsie likes to sleep.

K Stanyer (8)
Swaffham Bulbeck CE Primary School, Swaffham Bulbeck

Drone Hedgehog

D rops from a plane
R obot wings, robot wings
O n Saturday, he saves the day
N o one gets in his way
E veryone and anyone can't kill him

H oping to win battles
E very day he is strong
D odging, swaying, diving
G oing to save the day, coming to save you
E lectrifyingly fast
H ope he will come
O bviously cute
G oing to make you safe.

Joshua Parker (8)
Swaffham Bulbeck CE Primary School, Swaffham Bulbeck

Bella The Gymnast

Bella is a gymnast
Bella wears a red suit
Red suit
Red, red suit
She loves to run
Bella loves to climb and colour
She loves to look good
And put on glittery bows to go to gymnastics
Bella is a very good dog
And loves to go to gymnastics
She can talk
Today she is going to a big show
She is a girl and she can giggle
Bella can reads books
Bella is seven years old
She can write poems.

Avah Bailey (7)
Swaffham Bulbeck CE Primary School, Swaffham Bulbeck

Tim The Tortoise

T im the tortoise is my name and I like to eat
O ut in the garden is where I like to be.
R eaching for flowers and grass that I can see
T rouble is, I'm only tiny.
O liver is my owner, he loves me a lot
I love him, I really do.
S oil is what I play in and leaves are what I eat.
E very day I am happy to have a nice bath,
sometimes I accidentally fart, oops!

Oliver Arksey (8)
Swaffham Bulbeck CE Primary School, Swaffham Bulbeck

Police Chicken

Faster than racing cars.
Faster than cheetahs.
Zooming past everything
As fast as his wings can carry him.
The Police Chicken zooming round kerbs
Once he saw it, it was gone.
He saw parks and houses
It was all gone in a flap.
Going as fast as he can.
Chasing the bad guy.
Down the river dam
Going as fast as he can.
The bad guy ditches him
He flies into a tree.

Joshua Hedges (7)
Swaffham Bulbeck CE Primary School, Swaffham Bulbeck

Rose The Super Dog

Oh Rose, Rose, Rose, I love you so much
Sometimes you are a bit silly
But cute
Oh Rose, you just dropped your teddy
Oh Teddy, Teddy
Why are you so silly?
Rose, you are a superhero
Now you need to have more responsibility
I'm going to let you go
Bye, bye, bye
Rose found another superhero
It was lying down...

Jess Barber (7)
Swaffham Bulbeck CE Primary School, Swaffham Bulbeck

Raster's Acrostic Poem

R aster is good at skateboarding
A nd also, on ramps, he can ramp out of the Milky Way!
S uper speed, gives its shades food.
T hat means his shades change into a cooler form.
E nds those baddies with its cuteness!
R aster likes flights... sometimes. (Whispers) he accidentally fell out of a plane!

Xavier Kirkby (8)
Swaffham Bulbeck CE Primary School, Swaffham Bulbeck

Melvin The Silly Cat

M elvin surfed on the sea,
E ats tuna, fish and birds
L ovely Melvin, you're so silly, you
V anish into thin air and go back to surf
I love you so much, you're smooth, cute and silly
N othing else needed to make you cute, you're
also sweet, cuddly and sometimes spooky.

Melody Speed (7)
Swaffham Bulbeck CE Primary School, Swaffham Bulbeck

Chubby Chicken

A chicken that loves pancakes
He's called Chubby Chicken.

Chubby Chicken is very lazy and messy
Wild and tiny chicken.

Chubby Chicken has a cape
And wears glasses.

Chubby Chicken's favourite hobby
Is skateboarding.

Chubby Chicken can fly
But only with his cape.

Amber Smith (8)
Swaffham Bulbeck CE Primary School, Swaffham Bulbeck

The Skateboarding Goldfish

Oh, I'm sorry, I'm too busy
Bombing around on my skateboard.
Hi, I'm Bob.
I like bombing around on my skateboard,
Of course I play Fortnite!

And I'm a goldfish.

I wear sunglasses,
I am a cool dude,
I'm a gangster.

Once, I went to space with my skateboard.

Oscar Deistler (7)
Swaffham Bulbeck CE Primary School, Swaffham Bulbeck

Hairy The Horse

Hairy the horse always snorts.
He has long hair like a bear.
He is clever.
He has a bike and he doesn't bite.
He plays football and he's really good.
He lives in a house like a mouse.
He is lazy.
He wears a hat.
He is messy like Miss Jessy.
He's sometimes grumpy, his rocks are lumpy.

Hazel Weaver (9)
Swaffham Bulbeck CE Primary School, Swaffham Bulbeck

The Super Tortoise

S o cute
U nusual
P eculiar
E xtraordinary
R ound

T iny
O bviously very cute
R idiculously sassy
T erribly slow
O bviously very hungry
I t's fun with him!
S o happy
E very day he eats leaves!

Molly Sutherland (8)
Swaffham Bulbeck CE Primary School, Swaffham Bulbeck

There Was A Kitten Called Jasmine

J elly is her favourite food
A black little cat who loves snoring
S he loves her electric scooter
M elts in the sun
I n a crazy house with a very flexible body
N ail - "A long nail is what I need to tickle people."
E ndings of stories is what she loves!

Sophie Fenton (7)
Swaffham Bulbeck CE Primary School, Swaffham Bulbeck

The Rogue Hamster

There once was a hamster, a hamster, a hamster
He lived in a plane, a plane, a plane
He liked to skateboard, to skateboard, to skateboard
He likes to skydive, to skydive, to skydive
He eats burgers, eats burgers, eats burgers
It's the end, the end, the end.

Sidney Riethoff (8)
Swaffham Bulbeck CE Primary School, Swaffham Bulbeck

Tiger The Hamster

T iny little Tiger.
I am Tiger, I am a hamster.
G inger hamster with black stripes, that is me.
E lla is my friend, she is a hamster too.
R oar! I am Tiger, I can go roar! I am so scary, roar!

Flossie (7)
Swaffham Bulbeck CE Primary School, Swaffham Bulbeck

The Amazing Cat

There once was a cat
A cat, a cat, a cat
Who loved to skateboard, skateboard
He always goes to a park
A park, a park, a park
A skatepark, a skatepark, a skatepark
What an amazing cat!

Fred Fernandez (8)
Swaffham Bulbeck CE Primary School, Swaffham Bulbeck

Magnificent Pets

Once, there was a cat
A cute, cute cat.
He loved heights.
He was not afraid, afraid, afraid
Because it was fun, fun, fun!
One day, he put on a cap
So he could fly.

Noah Poujardieu (7)
Swaffham Bulbeck CE Primary School, Swaffham Bulbeck

Duck Went To The Doctor

Duck went to the doctors
Duck came back
Duck came back loving acrobats.
People gasped when
Duck did a flip
Everyone thought
Duck was a quiet little chick.

Hester Rudkin (8)
Swaffham Bulbeck CE Primary School, Swaffham Bulbeck

Wild Milly

W onderful
I ncredible
L oud
D ense

M uddy
I ncredibly
L ovely,
L oved
Y oung.

Sophie Grant Berry (8)
Swaffham Bulbeck CE Primary School, Swaffham Bulbeck

Coco The Kitten

C oco is beautiful she is cute.
O bedient is not a word in her dictionary.
C oco is very, very cute.
O bedient she's not, but I still love her.

T he cute cat is adorable.
H owever small she is, she will grow.
E ven when I am at school, I feel she's there.

K ittens are very adorable.
I love that mischievous fellow.
T he cute things that she does.
T en weeks old she is.
E very day, when we have toast, Coco eats the crumbs.
N ow I really want to cuddle her.

Makenzie Hope (9)
William MacGregor Primary School, Tamworth

Flopsy Rabbit

F lopsy was a fluffy rabbit
L oving, gentle and kind
O nly one ear and no tail had he
P ink was his nose
S ilver was his fur
Y ummy food he loved

R unning and jumping are his favourite sports
A ll of the races he wanted to win
B ut only having one ear,
B ertie Bunny he didn't hear coming
I n and out of the bushes Bertie dashed
T ripping and tumbling, Flopsy fell, rolling down,
he hit the winning bell!

Amelia Watson (7)
William MacGregor Primary School, Tamworth

The King Of Lizards

A peculiar pet doesn't get odder than mine
S caly like a dinosaur
I ndependent
A fly eater
N umber-one lizard

W ater giant
A six-foot monster
T ail swiping
E ggs are its babies
R azor-sharp teeth

M ischievous
O vereater
N oble lizard
I nsect eater
T errifying
O ld-looking
R estless animal.

Lydia Dennis (9)
William MacGregor Primary School, Tamworth

The Rhino That Can Shoot Lasers

The rhino shot his lasers all day.
He hit trees and bushes and hay.
The other animals thought he was dangerous
Though he was good.
Rhino did a laser show
For the other animals.
They laughed and clapped
And all became friends.

Alfie Allen (7)
William MacGregor Primary School, Tamworth

YOUNG WRITERS INFORMATION

We hope you have enjoyed reading this book – and that you will continue to in the coming years.

If you're a young writer who enjoys reading and creative writing, or the parent of an enthusiastic poet or story writer, do visit our website **www.youngwriters.co.uk**. Here you will find free competitions, workshops and games, as well as recommended reads, a poetry glossary and our blog. There's lots to keep budding writers motivated to write!

If you would like to order further copies of this book, or any of our other titles, then please give us a call or order via your online account.

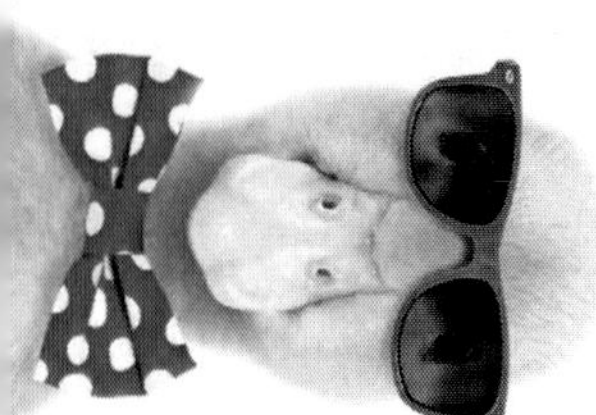

Young Writers
Remus House
Coltsfoot Drive
Peterborough
PE2 9BF
(01733) 890066
info@youngwriters.co.uk

Join in the conversation!
Tips, news, giveaways and much more!

YoungWritersUK

@YoungWritersCW